桂林风情
BEAUTIFUL GUILIN

漓江出版社

序

在地球东经110°、北纬25°处，有一块被称为山水甲天下的神奇之地，这就是桂林。

桂林地属亚热带季风气候，这里四季分明，气候宜人，雨量充沛，冬无严寒，夏无酷暑，有着"五岭皆炎热，宜人独桂林"的美誉。

"桂林山水甲天下"的赞誉早已使桂林的奇山秀水名声在外，这里"山清、水秀、洞奇、石美"，而如梦似幻的百里漓江更是桂林山水风光的精华所在，她的每一个视角都有一幅秀丽的风景画，令骚人墨客诗兴大发，让游览者赞叹不已。

神奇的土地养育着聪慧的人们，聪慧的人们热爱着神奇的土地。生活在这片神奇的土地之上的各族人民，以他们的勤劳智慧装扮美丽家园，以各具特色的淳朴民俗丰富山川自然。

踏上这片神奇的土地，不仅可以饱览如诗如画的山水风光，领略恬静美丽的田园风光，还可观赏到奇特的村寨风情和各少数民族奇异的民族风俗，体味到山野之间古朴的情趣和纯美的风情。

Prelude

Situated between 110° east longitude and 25° north latitude,Guilin has been well acclaimed as a magical land with the most beautiful landscape in the world.

Belonging to the subtropical monsoon region,Guilin enjoys a clear distinction of seasons and mild climate with sufficient rainfall.It is neither too hot in summer nor too cold in winter,just as a famous poet put it "When it is scorchingly hot everywhere in the five ridges,only Guilin has temperate weather."

The beautiful natural wonders with verdant mountains,elegant waters,magnificent crags and fantastic caverns has brought Guilin the fame abroad as well as at home.Lijiang River,more like an extending picture,winding its way among green mountains and villages from north to south,is the highlight of a completion of Guilin tour.The varied natural scenery along the river fills the tourists with imaginationsand wonder.

This magical land has been neutering generations of diligent people of various nationalities while people in turn,hand in hand,has been using their wisdom and working hard to have create colorful and sparkling cultures and to make their homeland a better place.

On this land,you will enjoy the amenities of picturesque landscape,refreshing rural scenery and diversified minority cultures.

风　土　人　情

CONDITIONS AND CUSTOMS

　　生活在桂北的壮、汉、苗、瑶、侗等少数民族，有着各自独特的文化传统和风俗习惯，形成了丰富多彩、乐趣无穷的民族风情。当你走进这片土地，你不仅能饱览迷人的山水风光，还可以领略那奇异的风俗，感受少数民族的古朴、豪放和热情。那绚丽的服饰、悦耳的歌声、多姿多彩的舞蹈、奇异的风俗，构成了一幅幅色彩斑斓的民族风情画卷。

　　The north of Guangxi autonomous region is a gathering place for ethnic minority groups such as Zhuang,Han,Miao,Yao and Dong etc each with its distinctive traditions and customs.Their long-time cohabitation on this land has created a colorful and interesting local culture.When you set your foot on this land,you can not only feast your eyes with picture-like landscape,but also taste the fantastic traditions and customs,sense the simplicity,freedom and hospitality of the locals.Colorful dresses,melodious tunes,bold

1.红帆远映

Sail on the horizon

赤い帆が遠く映つる

홍반원영

un reflet lointain d'une voile rouge

Ein rotes Segel fern im Fluß

la vela rossa rispecchiata sul fiume in lontananza

美丽的漓江，渔民们世世代代在这里休养生息。
Beautiful Lijiang River has been nurturing
generations of fishermen.

2.燃灯捕鱼
Lighting for fishing
灯火をつけて魚をとる
연등포어
la pêche au lamparo
Licht anzünden zum Fischfang
la pesca sotto lampada accesa

点亮马灯，可照见水中鱼儿，鱼鹰潜入江中，便可捕获鲜美的漓江鱼。
With the help of the dim light of oil lamp,cormorants dive into water and catch delicious fish.

傲立于老渔翁肩头的鱼鹰，显
示出它与渔翁非凡的亲密关系。
Flapping its wings
leisurely on the fisherman's
shoulder,the cormorant is
expressing their harmony
between them.

3.渔翁与鱼鹰
Old fisherman and his cormorant
漁夫と鵜
어부와가마우지
un pêcheur et son cormorant
Fischer und Kormorane
i pescatori ed i cormorani

4.船　炊
Boat cooking
漁船での炊煙
밥짓는배
la cuisine au bateau
Das Kochen im Schiff
la cottura dei pescatori

当晨曦初现，河畔船头便燃起炊火，这是渔家妇女在打点她们一家美味的早餐。

In early morning, women start a new day by preparing a delicious breakfast for the whole family.

5. 漓江渔火
Fishing boats and lights
灘江の漁火

이강어불
les lampes des pêcheurs sur le Li
Fischerlichter im Li-Fluß
la pesca con i cormorani sul fiume
Lijiang

破晓之时，静谧的江面上，起早的渔夫们
早已燃起了渔火，准备撒鱼网，捕捉他们一天
的希望。

It is dawning,on the quiet river,early
fishermen light up their lamps and get
ready to cast.

6.蓑翁织网

An old fisherman in coir raincoat weaving a fishnet

笠を被つている老漁夫が魚網を編む

그물만드는 로인

un tissage de filet des pêcheurs

Der Fischer bei der Knüpfarbeit

un vecchio pescatore faccendo il rammendo della rete

勤劳质朴是漓江之畔打鱼人家的传统美德。看，这位披蓑戴笠的老渔翁在小憩之时仔细地编织着他至爱的鱼网。

Industry is a fine value of fishermen on Lijiang River. The old fisherman in the picture in coir raincoat is carefully weaving a fishnet upon a rest.

7. 渔家少女晒鱼网

Fish girl spreading out her fishnet to dry

漁家の少女が魚網を乾す

거물말리는 어녀

les jeunnes filles sêchent des filets de pêche

Eine junge Fischerin beim Trocknen der Netze

una ragazza facendo l'essiccazione della rete da pesca al sole

8. 风 帆

Sails

帆掛け船

돛단배

la voile

Rote Segel

la vela

在沙滩上晾干鱼网，以防鱼网腐坏，也可方便补网。

Drying fishnets on the shoal regularly is done to prevent them from decaying and mend them in case of cracks.

漓江上用以运输的客船。

Passenger boats on Lijiang River.

9.漓江渔童

Fish boy on Lijiang River

灕江の小さい漁夫

이강어동

les enfants des pêcheurs sur le Li

Fischerknaben im Li-Fluß

un bambino del pescatore del fiume Lijiang

走进美妙的漓江，就像走进梦幻般的童话世界。

To sail along the beautiful Lijiang River is to enter a fairyland.

10. 清早撒网

Morning cast

明け方に魚網を放す

새벽그물치다

jeter des filets au point du jour

Netze auswerfen frühmorgens

la pesca con la rete al mattino

清早，渔夫在恬静的河面上撒开
鱼网，谱出一首幽美的波光曲。

The spreading fishing net
composes a melody on the glittering
water.

11.围 捕

Siege

魚を取りこめて取る

포위

la pêche au encerclement

Die Ringwadenfischerei

i cormorani circondando
per pescare i pesci

　　每每碰到鱼群，渔夫们总能
团结一致，四面包抄，一网打尽。
　　In case of a shoal of
fish,fishermen will cooperate
and catch them all.

12. 黄昏渔火

Lights in the dusk

夕方の漁火

황혼어불

les lampes des pêcheurs à la tombée de la nuit

Fischerlichter in der Abenddämmerung

la pesca con i cormorani al tramonto

夜幕降临，渔民们又忙着点亮马灯，围捕着江中的鱼儿。

Night approaching, fishermen go fishing with the burning oil lamps.

13.捕　获
Capture
捕　獲
포　획
le rendement de la pêche
Fischfang
aver preso il pesce con successo

　　鸬鹚、又名鱼鹰、是江中捕鱼的能手。
Cormorants are natural fish catchers on the river.

14.倾诉衷情
Confiding
衷情を訴える
경소애정
l'épanchement du coeur
Liebesgeplänkel
riversare I'affetto

15. 呵 护
    Guadians
    愛 護
    보 호
    les soins domesdiques
    Fürsorge für die Brut
    una difesa gentile

16. 仰天长啸
    Screeching into the sky
    天を仰いで長く鳴く
    앙천장하
    hurler
    Krähen zum Himmel
    cantare verso il cielo

17.憩
In peace
小　憩
휴　식
un repos
Eine Rast
il riposo

打鱼归来，鱼鹰们拍拍身上
的水珠，美美地休息一会儿。
Flapping off the water
drops leisurely,the cormorants
are enjoying a peaceful break
after fishing.

18.龙脊魂
Longji (the Dragon's Backbone) spirit
龍勝の魂

롱길혼

l'âme de la montagne du dos de dragon
Der Bauerngeist auf dem Terrassenfeld
I'anima di Longji

生活在龙脊山寨里的壮、侗、瑶家，因山田狭长，至今仍使用人拉犁这种古老的劳作方式，辛勤地耕耘着龙脊这块美丽的土地。

Zhuang,Dong and Yao are Minority ethnic groups living among the Dragon's Backbone terraces.Plough,a farming tool developed long time ago,remains to be the only practical tool of farming on terraces due to the special local topography.

19.织　锦
Weaving brocade
錦を織る

적면

tisser des brocarts
Brokat weben
la tessitura del broccato

　　织锦是瑶族民间传统工艺之一。瑶族姑娘擅长飞针走线，她们用色彩鲜艳的丝线、绒线编织出各种图案。其花鸟虫鱼、飞禽走兽优美生动，工艺精湛。

　　Brocade weaving has been one of the major fine arts of Yao people.Yao girls are born expert embroidery weavers.Under their skillful hands,flowers,birds or animals are all vividly presented.

20.捶　布
Hammering cloth
木槌で布を打つ

다듬질

frapper le tissu
Baumwollstoff klopfen
battere i panni

　　侗家所穿衣物皆为自织自染。在经过织、染、捶染、浣洗、晾晒等复杂的工序后，就可以缝制成衣。

　　Dong people make their clothes all by themselves.Completion of clothes making is a complex process including weaving,dying,hammering,washing and drying.

21. 秋　收
Harvest
秋の収穫

추수

la moisson d'automne

Herbsternte

il raccolto autunnale

　　龙胜山地坡度很大，独特的自然地理
条件决定了世居的龙胜各族人民在这里开
垦种地，层层梯田绕山转，这是龙胜的自
然景观。

　　Longsheng is situated among steep
mountains.Its unique geographic
conditions have decided on its unique
way of farming.The terrace fields
spiraling up around the mountains are
Longsheng's natural spectacle.

22. 金秋之舞
Dancing to the golden autumn
錦秋の踊り

추수춤

la dance d'automne

Im goldenen Herbst

l'essiccazione del riso
appeso sull'intelaiatura

　　生活在龙胜山寨里的瑶族和侗族，通常
以木头搭起高架晾晒稻穗，每当秋收后，村
寨里随处可见一排排金色的屏风。

　　In harvest season,Yao and Dong
people living in Longsheng's mountainous
villages erect walls of wood rails for
the purpose of drying harvested
crop.Those "golden screens" are a
pleasant view of the season.

23. 收获的喜悦
The joy of harvest
収穫の喜び
수확의 기쁨
la joie de rendement
Die Freude an der Ernte
la gioia del raccolto

　　龙胜山寨里的壮家，在稻谷收割晾晒好后，以这种特制的木槌工具进行脱谷。
　　Specially made wood hammer is the tool that Zhuang people use to thresh the dried grain.

24. 芬芳的晒台
Fragrant yard
芳しい物干し台
일광건조대
la sécherie parfumée
Die Trocknenfläche auf dem Dach
il terrazzino fragrante

　　烈日下，聪慧细心的壮家妇女正将一把把谷穗整理翻晒。
　　In the sunshine, the bright Zhuang women are carefully arranging the drying grain on the sunning ground.

25. 又是一年秋满楼
Another harvest year
もう一年の金色の豊収
역시추만류년
la maison pleine d'automne
Die Ernte in der Sonne
un altro anno del raccolto autunnale

　金秋时节，桂北人民的楼居里里外外满是金色的"秋诗"。
　In the golden season,the attics of Northern Guangxi people are filled up with "the verses of autumn".

26. 晴　日
Sunny day
晴れの日
청일
le jour ensoleillé
Ein sonniger Tag
il giorno sereno

　　小小年纪,已经成为父母劳动的好帮手。
　　Young as it is,the little girl is a helping hand to her parents.

27. 秋 实
Fruitful autumn
秋の実
구 실
le rendement d'automne
Herbstfrüchte
i meloni e frutti maturi in autunno

"麻栏"楼上，丰硕的秋实让壮家
妇女眉开眼笑。

The two Zhuang women on the
sunning porch beam at each other
over the bumper crop.

28. 舂 辣 椒
Pounding chilies
唐辛子を搗く
고추 찧다
écraser le piment
Paprika zerstoßen
polverizzare i peperoni nel mortaio

　利用一种古老的工具，侗家妇女密切配
合，勤快地舂着火红的辣椒。

　By ancient means, the two Dong women
work closely with each other in pounding
chilies.

29. 舂　米
Pounding grain
米を搗く
쌀찧다
décortiquer le riz
Reis mit Stößel und Mörser schälen
polverizzare il riso nel mortaio

利用碓具，类似于杠杆原理，一人踩在碓尾，前端则相应抬起，松开脚后则前端也相应落下，卯于碓身的木杵则舂入放有稻谷的石臼里，另一人用竹竿拨动石臼里的稻谷，如此循环往复，直到谷壳完全脱剥为止。

Treadle-operated tilt hammer is an instrument for hulling rice.It works on a similar basis of leverage.When one person steps on and off the end side of the hammer,the head side will be lifted and dropped accordingly,thus enabling the force of the head side ,joined with a wood pestle work on the grain contained in the big stone mortar.Near the head end stands the other person who helps stir the grain after each round of pounding.The pounding process will be continued repeatedly until the grain is well hulled.

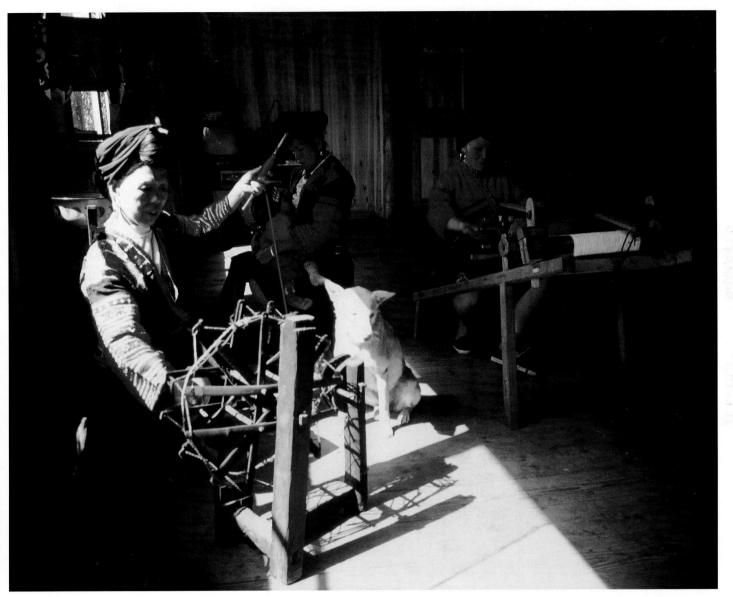

30.锦绣生活
Weaving out a brocade of life
錦の生活
금수생활
une vie merveilleuse
Spinnen und weben
la vita splendida

红瑶妇女正在使用古老的机器，以古老的方式编织她们美丽的服装。

The Hong Yao women are weaving their beautiful clothing with ancient looms in an ancient way.

31.禾廊岁岁满金谷

Golden screens

禾廊の収熟

해마다금수확

le grenier est rempli du riz toutes les années

Reisbündel überall

l'intelaiatura piena di riso dorato

　　每到金秋时节，当您踏着青石板小路走进乐江乡的地灵侗寨，随处可见金谷满挂的禾廊，阵阵稻香随风扑鼻而来，丰收的喜悦溢满了侗家。

　　In harvest season,when you enter Diling Dong village,you will be greeted with views of golden haystacks,wind with crop fragrance and the harvest joy pervading the whole village.

32.苗家之夜
Night in the Miao village
ミョウ家の夜

묘가의밤
une nuit chez les MIAOS
Die Nacht der Bauernfamilien
la notte della famiglia della minoranza Miao

入夜了，在明亮的灯光下，农家主妇还在用风谷机风净谷物。

Night falling, the village women are using land-operated wind blower to blow off the chaff in the grain in the bright light.

33.踏雪而归
Return in the snow
雪を踏んで帰ってくる
탑설귀환
au retour sous la neige
Die Rückkehr im Schnee
il rientro segnando il
passo sulla neve

冰天雪地之间，一位瑶族妇女
顾不上寒冷，扛着柴火，直奔家居。
Firewood on shoulder,the
Yao woman is anxiously heading
home against the falling snow.

34.团结就是力量

Unity is strength

団結は力である

단결은 힘이다

I'union fait la force

Einigkeit macht stark

L'unione fa la forza

秋收过后，龙胜各族自治县各族群众常在农闲之际，砍伐松树建新房，这是和平乡黄洛村的瑶族同胞抬树的情景。

People living in Longsheng often make use of the slack after autumn harvest to cut down big pine trees for the purpose of building new houses.This is the scene that the fellow villagers of Huangluo village of Heping county are carrying a big log.

35.磨
Grinder
石臼
갈다
un moulin
Mahlen
il mulino

　　磨是中国民间一种古老的生产工具，至今桂北地区人民仍普遍使用该生产工具进行劳作，用于磨米、磨豆腐等。
　　Grinder is an ancient tool of production.It is still widely used in northern Guangxi for·grinding rice or beans for making tofu.

36.编织生活

Weaving a beautiful life

織物による生活

편직생활

tisser une vie

Die Flechtarbeit

intrecciare la vita

　　竹编是桂北劳动人民的拿手好戏，是许多人家的重要收入来源，认真地编好每一个竹具，就是编织他们美好的生活。

　　People of Northern Guangxi are all expert weavers on bamboo wares.For many households it is still a primary income source.By weaving each ware skillfully they are weaving in their hopes for a bright future.

37. 捞取趴石鱼
Dredging for Stonefish
趴石魚を取る
바석어잡아올리다
pêcher
Ein Alter beim Fischfang
pescare i pesci

"捞取趴石鱼，夜来送好酒"。趴石鱼是龙胜各族自治县的著名土特产，它芳香味美，深受各族群众的喜爱，是招待贵宾的珍品。每到盛夏，龙胜480余条溪河，随处可以看到人们在打捞趴石鱼的身影。

Stonefish (a kind of fish) is a well-known local specialty of Longsheng county. It has a special flavor and tastes delicious,just as a saying has put it "Stonefish dredged up in the day,mellow wine matched at night." It is often used to entertain guests.In the height of summer,people searching for stonefish can be seen along each of Longsheng's 480 or more streams and rivers.

38. 壮妹采茶忙
Zhuang sisters busy with tea picking
チワン族の少女が忙しくて茶を摘む

분망히 차 체잡하는 장매
les jeunnes filles des ZHUANGS cueillent le thé
Junge Teepflückerinnen der Zhuang-Nationalität
le ragazze della minoranza Zhuang impegnate in raccolta di tè

龙脊茶是龙脊四宝之一，每年谷雨节后，布谷鸟鸣唱枝头，壮家姑娘就成群地上山坡采摘鲜嫩的茶芽，制成清新爽口的名茶。龙脊茶叶在乾隆年间就已是皇帝指定的贡茶，如今仍是全国二十八大名茶之一。

Longji tea is one of the four Longji treasures. Each year after the Grain Rain (the 6th of the 24 lunar terms), Zhuang girls in groups are seen spreading among tea bushes on hillsides picking up tea leaves to make the famous Longji tea. Longji tea was designated as tribute tea during the reign of Emperor Qianlong of Qing Dynasty. It still ranks among the nation's most famed 28 teas to date.

39.侗族百家宴

Dong people's hundred-household feast

トン族の百家の宴

동족백가연

un banquet de cent familles chez les DONGS

Ein Festessen im Dorf der Dong-Nationalität

un banchetto di cento famiglie della minoranza Dong

龙胜各族自治县乐江乡地灵村的侗族群众，每到关公(关羽)生日(农历六月廿四日)那天，都要集中在村边的风雨桥上，杀猪宰牛，拿出家中珍藏的酸鱼、酸鸭和糯米、水酒等，举行盛大的宴会。团结、好客、共谋致富方略，已成为村中的传说，如今古风依旧。

Each year on the day of Guangong's (a hero during The Three Kingdoms period) birthday which is 24th of the sixth lunar month.All the Diling villagers from Lejiang county,Longsheng gather before the village's wind-rain bridge to feast,each bringing to the banquet the best dishes from his home such as pickled fish,duck etc.Unity,hospitality and working closely for a better life are unchanged traditions of the village.

40.斗 马

Horse fighting

鬪 馬

두 마

le combat de cheval

Pferdekampf

un combattimento di cavalli

斗马是苗、瑶族人民的传统体育活动。相传这项活动源于一项婚姻的裁决，经过演变，斗马成为众人喜爱的群众性体育活动。每逢传统节日，苗、瑶人民都会进行斗马活动。

Horse fighting has been a traditional sport event of Miao and Yao people.Its origin can be traced back to a verdict on a marriage dispute.Over the years,it has evolved to be a popular sport event,an indispensable item on occasions of traditional festival.

41. 斗 牛

Bull fighting

鬪 牛

두 우

le combat de bufle

Stierekampf

un combattimento di bufali

斗牛是侗族人民最喜爱的娱乐活动之一，俗称"牛打架"。斗牛定在每年农历二月与八月的赶圩日进行。斗牛场一般选在侗寨的四面环山，可容纳万人以上的山谷或平坝中，也有的在专用的"打牛塘(水塘)"中进行，斗牛是力量的竞争，公平的竞赛，表达侗族人民庆贺风调雨顺，人畜兴旺。

Watching bull fighting is one of Dong people's favorite entertainments.The contest is usually held between the second lunar month and eighth lunar month.It is held on an open valley or a level grassland surrounded by mountains with a capacity of ten thousand viewers.Sometimes it is held in a specially chosen pool.Dong people's bull fighting reflects their sportsmanship and wishes for a prosperous year.

42.牛角号声

Ox horns

牛の角での演奏

우각호성

un cornet à bouquin

Die Hornbläser

il suono di tromba della corna del bue

牛角号是苗族的传统乐器之一，在节庆典礼
或重大的仪式上吹奏，声音雄浑悦耳。

　Ox horn is traditional music instrument
of Miao minority nationality.The vigorous
and firm sounds are usually heard on festival
ceremonies or various important events.

43.壮族师公舞

Sorcerer dance

チワン族の「師公」踊り

장족사공무

la dance de sorcier des ZHUANGS

Shigong-Tanz der Zhuang-Nationalität

il ballo tradizionale di Shigong della
minoranza Zhuang

师公舞是壮族一种民间信仰活动，表演者戴莫
一大王傩面具，腰间系稻草裙，模仿青蛙动作进行
表演，以祈求稻作丰收。

Sorcerer dance is a worship activity among
the Zhuang people.Wearing masks of King Moyi
and hay skirts on hips,the performers dance
to imitate frogs to prey for a good harvest.

44.娶 亲

Getting married

嫁を迎える

장가 들다

un mariage

Die Heirat

ammogliarsi

桂北山区的少数民族在生活中形成了独特的迎娶婚俗。在娶亲的当日，青年男女将事先准备好的喜猪、酒、糯米等送至女方，迎亲队伍约三十多人，吹吹打打，喜气洋洋。

The Minority groups in the Northern Guangxi area have shaped their own marital customs.On the wedding day,groom's family forms a team of around thirty people to escort the prepared betrothal gifts to the bride's family.The gifts include pig,wine,rice etc.On the march,marrying tunes will be played all along the way to create a jubilant air.

45.瑶家婚礼

Yao style marriage

ョウ家の婚礼

요가혼례

un mariage des YAOS

Die Hochzeit der Yao-Nationalität

una cerimonia matrimonia della minoranza Yao

瑶族缔结婚姻的形式主要有两种：一是嫁女要媳，另一种是招郎入赘，不论何种形式，结婚典礼都是隆重热闹的。

There are two ways for a Yao couple to get married and live their married life:one is for the woman to marry into and live with the groom's family,the other instead is for the man to marry into and live with the bride's family.Either way taken,the wedding is a grand ceremony.

46. 侗家美酒醉千客

The intoxicating Dong watery wine

トン家の美酒が千人の客を酔っ払わせられる

천객을 취하는 동가술

le bon vin des DONGS enivre les invités

Der gute Reiswein der Dong-Nationalität

i clienti ubriachi dal buon vino nella famiglia della minoranza Dong

龙胜侗乡的水酒是以优质糯米为原料酿造，醇香可口，意味深长，这是玉龙滩风情园的侗族敬酒舞。

High quality glutinous rice is the major material for brewing Dong watery wine. The wine is full and mellow with a lingering flavor. This is the scene of Dong villagers' Toast Dance.

47. 侗乡闹春牛

Bull dance of Dong village

トン族の「春の牛」上演

입춘을 맞이하는 동족향

le bufle réveille le printemps

Ochsentanz im Dorf der Dong-Nationalität

l'animazione primaverile dei bufali nel villaggio della minoranza Dong

　　每年立春这天，龙胜平等侗乡都要闹春牛，用这种形式向众人报春，昭示人们春天来了，一年之季在于春，不要误了农时。春牛舞到侗寨的每一个岩坪，招来众人的观看，热闹非凡。

　　Bull dance is performed on the day marking the beginning of the 1st lunar term (Feb. 3,4,or5) to celebrate the coming of spring in various Dong villages of Longsheng.It symbolizes that the spring has come and it is the most important time for farm work and that people should make good use of it.Everywhere that the bull dance reaches,it is a jubilant scene.

48.芦笙踩堂
   Lu-Sheng totem pole
   芦笛柱の上演
   피리소리 발짜국소리
   la dance avec l'instrument musical LUSHENG
   Tanz nach Lusheng-Musik
   il ballo tradizionale di Lusheng

每逢苗年或盛大节日，苗寨男女老少均要围绕芦笙进行吹笙踩堂。芦笙柱色彩斑斓，柱子顶端立着一只面朝东方的白寒鸡模型，中间有一对牛角模型，柱子上雕着一条盘绕的龙，柱子底座形如铜鼓。芦笙柱高达两丈以上。竖柱时，男女老少均围绕其吹笙踩堂，热闹一番。

Upon each Miao year or grand occasion,the whole Miao village,old or young,come dancing and playing Lu-Sheng (reed-pipes,a musical instrument) around a colorful totem pole.The pole is 2 *zhang* (a unit of length which is equal to $3\frac{1}{3}$ meters) long,stands on a pedal in the shape of a bronze drum.The body of the pole is surrounded with a dragon with a white chicken model facing the east on the top and a pair of ox horn model in the middle.

49.芦笙阵阵传山寨
The Resounding Lu-Sheng
芦の笛声が山寨の中で木霊する
산이울매 울리는 피리소리
la mélodie de LUSHENG résonne
dans le village
Lusheng-Musik im Bergdorf
suonare lo strumento musicale di
Lusheng

　龙胜各族自治县乐江乡西腰村
的侗族芦笙队，常常到邻近村寨进
行友情演出。
　Xiyao village's Lu-sheng
(reed-pipe) performance team is
performing for the neighbor
villages.

50. 竹竿舞

Bamboo pole dance

竹竿の踊り

대나무춤

la dance de canne de bambou

Tanz mit den Bambusstöcken

il ballo delle canne di bambù

竹竿舞又称"打柴舞"、"打竹舞",原是黎族民间舞蹈形式之一,后成为桂北山区许多少数民族迎宾的舞蹈之一。

Bamboo dance, dubbed as "firewood beating dance" or "bamboo pole beating dance" started as one of Li minority nationality's major dance forms, has now become a dance form to receive guests among various minority ethnic groups of northern Guangxi area.

51. 傩　戏
God drama
傩戲（神劇）
귀신쫓기
la dance d'accueil de dieu
Die lokale Oper mit Masken
il ballo tradizionale d'esorcismo di Nuoxi

傩戏，又称神剧，据说起源于春秋时期，至今已有二千七百年的历史，多在酬神还愿或祭祀活动时演出。一般由一至三人头戴面具，身着草衣，模拟各种动作进行表演，以驱鬼祭神。此外傩戏还吸收彩调一些声腔，运用联曲手法演唱，使形式更加丰富多彩。

God drama,or god opera, is said to have started in the Spring and Autumn period and it has had a history of two thousands seven hundred years. It is performed on the occasions of preying to or worshiping gods. It features one to three people or more wearing masks and cloaks dancing in imitation of certain behaviors to drive away ghosts and worship gods. God opera has been greatly enriched by taking in some operatic tunes of local opera of Guangxi and the way to sing tunes ,jointly.

52. 打 油 茶
Oily tea
油茶を作る

차기름 짜다

préparer le thé à l'huile
Den Tee mit Öl kochen
cuocere il tè d'olio

　　打油茶是桂北山区的侗、苗、瑶等民族一种特有的饮食习惯。油茶通常用糯米、茶油、茶叶制成，再加上炒米花、炒花生、炸油果等配料，香醇可口，可以提神醒脑，祛寒暖胃。图中为龙胜红瑶几家人围在火炉旁打油茶的情景，油茶飘香，其乐融融。

　　Making oil tea is a daily necessity for a mixture of minority ethnic groups living in northern Guangxi, among which are Dong, Miao and Yao. The major materials to make oil tea are glutinous rice, camellia oil and tealeaves. Other ingredients like fried peanuts are eaten together with the oily tea to give it additional fun and flavor. Eating oil tea often can help rid off cold and warm stomach. This is the gathering of several households enjoying the pleasure of making and eating oily tea.

53.炊
Cooking
炊事
밤짓기
la cuisine
Das Kochen
la cottura

火红的炭火，阵阵的油茶香，母女俩甜蜜的笑容，预示着美好的未来。
Burning charcoal, pervading flavor of oily tea, sweet smiles symbolizing an auspicious future.

54．春节走亲家

Visit in the Spring Festival

春節に親戚の家へ挨拶に行く

설날천척방문

rendre visite chez les parents

Besuche im Frühlingsfest

una visita da parente durante la Festa di Primavera

走亲家是龙胜农村的传统习俗，一般是给亲家送一些酒肉、糍粑之类的食品。踏雪走亲家，别有一番情趣。

It is a tradition in rural Longsheng for the parents of a married child to pay a visit to his or her parents-in-law during the Spring Festival. The gifts are usually wine,rice cakes etc.The man in the picture is on her way to pay a visit while enjoying the

55. 火红的日子
Flaming life
真っ赤な暮らし
좋은날
une vie enrichie
Das glutrote Leben
i giorni prosperi

　生活在桂北山区的红瑶常以辣椒祛寒。每到辣椒收获的季节。红瑶村民就用长线将辣椒串起，挂在屋内火塘上方用火烘干，也可放在屋外让太阳晒干。

　Chilies are often used to drive away cold among Hong Yao ethnic group living in the mountainous area of northern Guangxi. When the chilies are harvested, they are stringed and hung up to dry off over an indoor fire or in the sunshine.

56. 包粽子
Making zongzi
粽子を作る
주악을 싸다
préparer un gâteau farci du riz
Klebreisklößchen mit Bambusblättern einwickeln
impacchettare il budino cinese

　　生活在桂北山区的红瑶，以糯米为主要粮食作物，粽子是主要食品之一。瑶族粽子有三角粽、五角粽、枕头粽等多种形状，每逢佳节或迎送宾客，均以粽子为送礼佳品。

　　Glutinous rice is staple food of the Hong Yao people in Northern Guangxi and it is often made into zongzi. According to the different shapes of zongzi when they are made, they can be divided into three pointed, five pointed and pillow shaped ones. Zongzi also constitute a good gift for friends and relatives.

57.打 糍 粑

Making rice cakes

糍粑を打つ

찹쌀떡만들기

frapper la pâte de riz glutineux

klebrige Reiskuchen machen

cuocere la pasta di riso glutinoso

　　打糍粑是桂北山区少数民族逢年过节的主要食俗之一。每到逢年过节，人们会将浸泡好的糯米蒸熟，放在粑石上用粑棰不断敲打，再将捶好的糯米揉捏成型晾干即可。

　　It is a major dietary custom to make rice cakes for northern Guangxi's minority groups during the lunar new year season. The glutinous rice, after being well immersed and steamed, is put into a big stone mortar. One or two persons pound on it with wood hammers until it is smashed into paste. Take out the paste, roll it into balls and then press them into cakes before leaving them to dry.

58.顶 竹 杠
Poking bamboo pole
竹竿の試合

대나무멜대
un jeu de bambou
Das Bambusstockspiel
far resistenza reciproca della canna di bambù

　　龙胜各族自治县泗水乡细门村的游戏——顶竹杠，是深受瑶族男女青年喜爱的游乐方式。通过顶竹杠，男女青年可以加强身体锻炼，增进感情，快乐愉悦，最后步入爱情的殿堂。

　　Pushing bamboo pole is a favorite entertainment for the youngsters of Ximen village, Sishui county of Longsheng. It is a healthy game in which young men and young women improve health, promotes mutual affection which may lead to a marriage.

59.舞 龙

Dragon dance

龍を舞う

무룡

la dance de dragon

Der Drachentanz

maneggiare il drago

关公文化节是恭城人民纪念三国时期名将关羽而举行的纪念活动，于1998年正式定名。关公节的纪念活动，一般每年农历六月十二日举行，主要活动有：关公出游、戏曲表演、舞龙舞狮、山歌对唱等。

Guangong Cultural Festival,authorized in 1998,is held by the Gongcheng people to commemorate Guangong, a well known officer during the Three Kingdom period (220-280).The relating activities,generally held on the 12th of the sixth lunar month annually including Guangong outing,opera performance,dragon dance,lion dance and singing folk songs etc.

60.舞　狮
Lion dance
獅を舞う
사자춤
la dance de lion
Der Löwentanz
maneggiare i leoni

61. 不让须眉

Heroic women

ドラゴンボートレース

수염과눈썹이길다

le courage féminin

Das Drachenbootsrennen der Frauen

non perdere nel confronto degli uomini

桂林自古就有"十年一大扒，五年一小扒"的龙舟竞赛风俗。每到端午节，漓江边各村紧锣密鼓，男女龙舟队如同水面飞龙，桨影如火雁展翅，四周掌声、喝彩声如歌，热闹非凡。

Guilin has a long history of holding dragon boat competition to celebrate the Dragon Boat Festival(the 5th of the fifth lunar month). The competition is held on the beautiful Lijiang River and it is divided into women's competition and men's competition. On that day, the competition scene is always turned into a bustling picture with crowds of people, riot of cries, laughter, applause etc.

62. 端午节盛况
A spectacle of the Dragon Boat Festival
端午節の盛况
단오절정경
la cérémonie solennelle de la fête de poète
Das Drachenbootfest
la grande occosione della Festa della Barca Dragone

巨大的龙船上人们载歌载舞，龙头烈焰喷发，极为壮观。

On the huge dragon boat are people singing and dancing while streams of flames are projecting out from the dragon's mouth.

63. 放 河 灯
Setting off lanterns
「河灯節」に河灯を放す

방하등

allumer des lampions dans la rivière

Festlampions in den Fluß

mandare via le lampade di fiume

农历七月十四俗称"鬼节"、人们都要举行祭祀先人活动。图为桂林资源县某地的人们举行的河灯节、通过放河灯来告慰先人、寄托对先人们的哀思、并祈求先人们保佑平安。

The 14th of the seventh lunar month is the "Ghost Festival". On this day, activities are held to worship the ancestors including releasing lanterns on rivers as shown in the picture taken in Ziyuan under the jurisdiction of Guilin. The lanterns are loaded with people's memory of their ancestors and the wishes to

64.山美，水美，发更美
Pretty mountains,pretty waters and pretty long hair
山が美しくて、水が綺麗で、少女の髪がもつと美しい
산미 수미 발긍미
les cheveux sont plus beuax que les monts et les eaux
Lange schöne Haare
le belle ragazze con i capelli lunghi della minoranza Hong Yao

被上海吉尼斯总部命名为长发村的龙胜各族自治县和平乡黄洛村，140余口人中，头发长度100厘米以上的妇女有60多人，妇女在河边结伴洗发成了一道亮丽的风景线。

Huangluo village, Heping country of Longsheng has been entitled by the Guinness World Records Shanghai headquater as Long Hair Village. Among a population of around 140, there are over 60 women with their hairs over 100 cm in length. The picture is a scenic view of women washing their hairs in the flowing water.

65.互 助

Mutual help

互いに助け合う

호조

une aide mutuelle

Die Haare einander waschen

aiutarsi l'un l'altro

长发是侗家女子的一种标志，洗发便成了她们互助友好的一种交流方式，清山秀水之间留下了她们亲密友好的足迹。

Long hair is a characteristic of Dong Girls. Helping each other in the washing and taking care of their long hair in green mountains and near clear waters is a way to communicate and promote friendship.

66.瑶家药浴
Yao's herbal bath
ヨウ家の薬の入浴

요족약욕
un bain médical des YAOS
Das Heilbad der Yao-Nationalität
un bagno medicinale nella famiglia della minoranza Yao

　　龙胜盘、红瑶族有药浴的习俗，这是常年生活在高山
密林中的瑶家为抵御湿气和风寒而发掘的民间药方。药浴
有防治风湿病、驱散疲劳的功效。
　　The Pan Yao and Hong Yao people living in
Longsheng have a habit of bathing in a huge bucket
with herbal medicines in it to cure and prevent
rheumatic pains and other diseases, or to get rid of
the tiredness after a day of hard work. This is due
to the fact that Yao people usually live in high and
humid mountainous areas.

67. 情　侣
Lovers
恋仲(アベック)

애인

侗家的男女青年，以弹琴、对歌的方式
互诉衷情。

Dong's young women and young men
express their affection for their
beloved ones through playing musical

68. "辣妹子"
Chili girl
辣妹子
라매자
une fille de piment
Ein Mädchen mit Paprika geschmückt
una "ragazzina piccante"

　　辣椒是壮乡之宝，为壮家的经济支柱来源，独特的土质、气候条件培育了独特的产品，每到椒红季节，壮家屋檐下挂满了串串红辣椒，顽童更是将之当作游戏乐园。

　　Chilies are Zhuang people's treasure which are their major income resource. The unique local conditions give special quality to them. After the harvest, strings of chilies hung under the eaves form a pleasing view and a playing ground for the kids.

69.迎春喜洋洋
Welcoming the Spring Festival
ほくほくと春節を迎える

득이양양히 봄맞이
I'accueil joyeux du printemps
Das fröhliche Frühlingsfest
raggiante di gioia per dare il

春节是桂北最为隆重的节日，贴春联、穿新衣、欢欢喜喜过大年，红红的大门贴着金色的福字，盛妆的小孩子提着红红的灯笼、红红的爆竹，吉祥的文字寄托着人们对来年的希望。

Spring festival is the most important traditional festival throughout the year for all the Chinese people including those of Northern Guangxi. Wearing new clothes, pasting spring festival couplets and golden "Fu" (happiness)onto the gateposts, door panels and doors are some of the major preparation activities

70.童 趣

Childhood happiness

子供時代の趣

동취

le goût d'enfant

Ein Kinderspiel

la gioia dei bambini

跳皮筋是桂北小朋友喜爱的一项娱乐活动，可单人跳、双人跳、多人跳，跳时先将皮筋套在两人脚下，后节节上升，直至无人跳上为止，是一项健身兼娱乐的游戏。

Rubber band skipping is a favorite sport for children of northern Guangxi. The game can involve varying number of members from three to more. The band is stretched straight by hooking up by two persons on the ankles. The game is upgraded by

71.祖 孙 乐
Harmonious grandfather and grandson
祖父と孫の幸せな時光
조손락
la joie du grand-pére petit-fils
Großeltern und Enkelkinder
la gioia tra nonno e nipote

　尊老爱幼是桂北各族人民的优良
传统、慈祥的老人、精致的摇篮、调皮
的孩童、加上室内朴实的摆设、构成
一幅普通而又温馨的画卷。

　Respecting the aged and caring
for the children is a traditional
virtue among the people living in
the northern Guangxi. The essence
of the virtue is well illustrated
by the warm family atmosphere
reflected from this picture
highlighting the kindly face of
the grandfather,naive child, well-
made cradle and those simple
settings.

72. 棋逢对手
Worthy matches
好敵手に合う
호적수를 만나다
le fervent du jeu des échecs
Das Schachspiel

在桂北的村村寨寨、门前路边随处可见
棋迷们摆下棋盘，进行着智慧的较量。

Playing chess is a popular game in
those big or small villages in northern
Guangxi. Anywhere from before the front
door to the side of the road can be a
"battle ground" for a contest in wisdom.

73. 旅游店面
Gifts and souvenir shops
土産屋

쇼핑가개

une boutique touristique
Der Laden für Touristen
un negozietto turistico

　　阳朔西街有一百多个专卖旅游品的店面，出售民族服饰、工艺品、瓷器、古玩等，为游客了解民族风情、开阔眼界、增长知识、收集民族纪念品提供了便利，为来桂林旅游游客必游之所。

There is a street called west street in Yangshuo which is flanked by over one hundred shops devoted to selling gifts and souvenirs. It is a must for all the tourists who come to Yangshuo for sightseeing. These shops boasts an excellent selection of goods including ethnic minorities dresses and adornments, art works, china wares, antiques etc. The existence of these shops helps the tourists to broaden their horizons and understand better about china's colorful minority cultures.

74.老 来 福
Peaceful old age
年寄りの楽しみ
로래복
une vieillesse heureuse
Das Glück einer alten Oma
un'anziana felice

　桂北民风淳朴，人民勤劳而善
良，古朴的大门上倒贴一个"福"字
寄托了人们对生活的企盼，古色的
石阶上坐着悠然自得的老人，构成
一幅朴实而又幸福的画卷。

　　The quaint door, the upside
down "Fu"(which means happiness
comes), the peaceful and content
old woman on the stair constitute
a expressive picture.

75.古老的浴场
Ancient bathing pool
古ム浴場

오랜욕장
un plage ancien
Ein altes Bad
una piscina antica

这是桂北农村常见的古老浴场、普通的围场阻隔着人们的视线、这里是男子自由的天地、是他们谈天说地、增进友谊、传授知识的场所。

This is one of the most common ancient bathing pools in northern Guangxi's rural area. A wall well surrounding the pool keeps the inside a free area for the men in bath to

76.瑶族顶板头饰
Yao nationality's hairstyle
ョウ族の「顶板」頭飾り

요족천판장식
la décoration de tête des YAOS
Der Kopfschmuck mit Platte der Yao-Nationalität
la decorazione di testa con soffitto della minoranza Yao

瑶族女子的顶板头饰，先梳发髻，用花巾缠头，再架上一个人字形的竹架，竹架上罩一块绣有花边的黑色头罩，头罩中间高高挺起，两边中幕垂挂，中间系珠旒。

Yao woman coils the hair into a bun, warps with a hem, tops with a "人" shaped bamboo frame. Covers the frame with a black cloth with flower patterns of embroidery on the edge. The middle front part of the head cover stands high with adornments, the fringe drops.

77.侗族妇女服饰

Dong women costumes

トン族の婦女服飾り

동족부녀복장

les costumes des femmes des YAOS

Die Damenkleidung der Dong-Nationalität

I'ornamento dell'abito da donna della minoranza Dong

侗族妇女习惯将长发梳辫，左右盘绕在头上，用木梳或银簪将造型别致的发型固定好，头上插花，胸前佩挂多层宽银圈，脖颈上套多重银项圈，手腕上套有银镯，整套装束绚丽多彩。

Dong women braid their hair and wear it in coils, shapes them into different styles with the help of combs and silver hairpins, puts on other accessories. Dong women's dresses are splendid with multi layers of silver medals and neckbands, silver bracelets.

78.盘瑶顶板高架头饰
Pan Yao women hairstyle
盤ョウ族の「頂板高梁」頭飾り
판요천반에높은장식
la décoration de tête haussée des YAOS
Der hohe Kopfschmuck der Yao-Nationalität
la decorazione di testa con soffitto in alta della minoranza Pan Yao

瑶族妇女最古老的头饰——顶板高架。这种装饰通常为头顶木板高架,外披饰瑶锦,向后垂帘至腰,两侧缀锦条串珠,十分引人注目。

This is the most ancient hairstyle for Pan Yao women. It is generally made so by wearing a wood frame on the head, covering it with a piece of colorful brocade which reaches down to the waist on the back. There are strings of beads and bands hanging from the two sides. It is very impressive.

79.盘瑶平头饰
Pan Yao women convenience hairstyle
盤ョウ族の平頭飾り

판요장식
la décoration plate des YAOS
Der flache Kopfschmuck der Yao-
Nationalität
la decorazione di testa in forma piana
della minoranza Pan Yao

　　盘瑶妇女平头饰由顶板高架饰演变
而来，为的是便于劳动。通常垂珠或彩丝
线，配以镶有斑斓瑶锦的黑色对开襟上
衣，色彩夺目，甚为漂亮。
　　This kind of hairstyle has
evolved from the high frame style
in response to the need of
convenience. It features dropping
strings of beads and multi-colored
silk threads. It goes best with a
black middle-buttoned undershirt
highlighted by the bright embroidery
that goes along the neckline.

80. 苗家长寿老人
Longest-living lady
ミョウ家の長寿の老人
묘가장수로인
un vieux MIAO avec longévité
Die alte Oma der Miao-Nationalität
un vecchio di longevità della minoranza Miao

苗族妇女传统头饰为蓄发盘缠螺蛳髻于脑后、插银簪、青巾包头、两鬓外佩有多种首饰。

Traditional hair style for the Miao women is to tie up the hair into a bun on the back of head and fix it with a silver hairpin, wrap the head with a green cloth and wear a variety of head ornaments on the two sides.

81. 红瑶服饰

Hong Yao costumes

红ョウ族の装身具

홍요복장

les costumes des YAOS rouge

Kleidung und Putz der Yao-Nationalität

I'ornamento dell'abito della minoranza Hong Yao

红瑶妇女喜爱穿玫瑰色的绣花衣，腰间扎鲜红色彩带，故名红瑶。其爱盘发，头发又黑又亮而且很长。幼儿戴的帽子饰物精致而复杂，很是亮丽。

Hong Yao gets its name "Hong" from its favor of rosy embroidery jacket with red belt. Hong Yao women have long dark hair which they coil up. The hat and ornaments the child wears showcase the sophistication of their handicraft.

82.瑶族女童服饰
　Girls
　ョウ族の女童服装
　요족여동복장
　les costumes de filles des YAOS
　Kleidung und Putz von Mädchen
der Yao-Nationalität
　I'ornamento dell'abito da bambina
della minoranza Yao

　　瑶族服饰丰富多彩，喜欢以彩色锦物作装饰，并缀以彩色绒丝线。图中瑶族小姑娘头上所佩银饰就是以红色锦条固定。黑色对襟开上衣镶有艳丽彩边，以腰带固定。腰带为瑶族男女老少常备之物，两端亦绣瑶锦缀彩成装饰。

　　Yao costumes are greatly diversified. It features bright colored embroidery as decorations. In the picture, the silver ornaments the girls wears on the head are fastened with red brocade banners, their black shirts have embroidered collars fastened on the waist by a embroidered belt with both ends dropping. Belts are important part of Yao costumes.

83.侗族男子服饰
　Dong men costumes
　トン族の男子の服装
　동족남자복장
　les costumes d'homme des DONGS
　Die Herrenkleidung der Dong-
Nationalität
　I'ornamento dell'abito da uomo
della minoranza Dong

　桂北侗族男子身着紫色衣，无
领斜襟宽袖，束腰带；下身紫布便
裤；头扎侗布头巾，赤脚。
　Dong men living in northern
Guangxi fancy purple collarless
shirts, loose sleeves, belts and
loose pants. Dong man wraps his
head with a piece of cloth and
is bare-footed.

84.瑶族男子服饰
Yao men costumes
ョウ族の男子の服装
요족남자복장
les costumes d'homme des YAOS
Die Herrenkleidung der Yao-
Nationalität
l'ornamento dell'abito da
uomo della minoranza Yao

瑶族男子传统服饰多为头巾以
青巾螺旋式缠于头上，上着青色上
衣，下着青布宽裤头，裤长齐膝。
Yao man wraps his head with
a piece of green cloth, wears a
green jacket and loose green
pants reaches down to the knees.

85. 侗家银项圈
Dong women's silver necklace
トン家の銀のネックレス飾り

동족은목걸이
le colier d'argent des DONGS
Silberne Halsreifen der Dong-Nationalität
la collana d'argento della minoranza di Dong

侗家妇女喜欢挂金戴银，首饰多种多样，其中最大最重的是银项圈。大的银项圈，从颈脖挂到腰部，重达四五公斤，式样也千差万别，不同年龄的妇女，式样也各不相同。

Dong women favor various gold and silver jewelry among which the most eye-catching is silver necklace. It hangs to reach the waist with varying weights. Some weigh 4 to 5 kg.The styles are varied in response to the different age groups.

田 园 秀 色

IDYLLIC COUNTRYSIDE SCENERY

在奇山秀水之间，处处是美丽的田园风光。点点村落，丛丛绿树，片片蔗林，块块稻田，或炊烟袅袅，或水气蒙蒙，或素霭如幔，或白雾如凝，或青云似带，每一片视野都是一幅元气淋漓的水墨画。置身于桂林的田园里，就像处在温柔之乡的梦里，有如优美的童话世界；置身于桂林的田园里，你会感到身心俱静，所有的烦恼、焦虑、急躁都会烟消云散，无影无踪，进入"物我两忘"的境界。

One will never enjoy the enchanting beauty of Guilin thoroughly without being inside the idyllic countryside scenery. Standing among the mass of green mountains and the elegant waters, overlooking the vastly extending fields, one feels becoming part of the great nature, and totally forget his own existence in a tender dreamland. In such a fabulous world, wherever our eyes reach, it is a vivid Chinese water and ink picture. Veil of mist over the distant mountains, patches of green rice fields, verdant woods, scattering villages and hovering smoke will melt away the harsh aspects of life and nourish the restless soul.

86.梯田·春魂
Terraces · Spirit of spring
だんだん畑 · 春の魂
다락밭 춘혼
des rizières en terrasse.l'âme de ptintemps
Das Terrassenfeld im Frühling
i campi a terrazze——l'anima primaverile

　龙胜梯田，层层叠叠，盘绕回环，直上云端，
春夏秋冬，景色各异，每个季节都显示出不同的
神韵。
　　Longsheng's terraces, layer over layer,
seemingly winding up to the sky offer you
changing views and feelings throughout the
seasons.

87.梯田 · 夏曲
Terraces· Song of summer
だんだん畑 · 夏の曲
다락밭 하곡
des riziéres en terrasse.mélodie d'été
Das Terrassenfeld im Sommer
i campi a terrazze——la conzone estiva

88. 梯田·秋染
Terraces·Golden tints
だんだん畑·秋の染め
다락밭 추란
des rizières en terrasse.teinture d'automne
Das Terrassenfeld im Herbst
i campi a terrazze──la tinta autunnale

89.梯田・冬雪
Terraces・In white
だんだん畑・冬の雪
다락밭 동설
des rizières en terrasse.neige d'hiver

90.如梦似幻
Dream or reality
夢ような感覚
환상같은꿈
les images oniriques
Im träumerischen Märchenland
il paese dei sogni

云雾迷蒙的春晨，远处的村寨及梯田淹
没于云雾之中，若隐若现，美妙异常，仿佛
处于仙境之中，令人拍手叫绝。

In early spring morning, distant
mountains, terraces on the hillsides,
villages are all immersed in fog and
clouds, obscure occasionally. Is this
reality or a dream?

91.春　耕
Spring ploughing
春　耕
봄갈이
le labour de printemps
Die Frühjahrsbestellung
la coltivazione primaverile

　　春天里，早起的劳动人民在耕耘着他们美
丽的家园。这是距桂林市南郊10公里处奇峰镇
一带田园。
　　Farmers are ploughing and sowing in
spring. The picture was taken in the rural
area 10 km south of Guilin city.

92.希望的田野
The fields of hope
希望の畑と野原
희망의 전야
des champs plein d'espoir
Das hoffnungsvolle Feld
la campagna della speranza

这是一个美丽的家园，更是一片希望的田野，茁壮的禾苗预示着农民们丰收的希望。

It is our homeland and it is more a land of hopes. The green and healthy crops promise a good harvest.

93. 农夫与牛
Peasant and buffalo
農夫と牛

농부와소
un paysan et son bufle
Der Bauer und seine Wasserbüffel
i contadini ed i bufali

烈日下，精神矍铄的老农敞开古铜色的胸怀，迈着沉稳的脚步，赶牛回家。

In the sunshine, a vigorous old peasant is driving home his buffalo.

94.世外桃源
Heaven of peace
ユートピア
세외도원
l'Eldorado
Im Traumland
il paradiso

山环水绕、田连阡陌、桃花遍野、绿竹幽径是"世外桃源"的一大特色。

Verdant mountains and elegant waters, extension of fields with crisscrossed paths, patches of peach blossoms are what we experience in the famous scenic spot "shi wai tao yuan" (a heaven of peace).

95.春 韵
Feeling spring
春の春めくこと

춘운
la rime de printemps
Die Frühlingsanmut
I`attrativa di primavera

云雾中青山如黛，江水涟涟，田野里一片翠绿，一片忙碌，这就是春天里阳朔田园的情趣。

　　Dark peaks in clouds, blue waters in continuity, green fields in extension, farmers in busy work are the rural amenities of Yangshuo in early spring.

96. 万点桂山尖
Riot of green peaks
桂山の奇観
만점계림산
pointus sont des milliers de pics
Tausende von grünen Gipfeln
i pinnacoli innumerevoli delle colline di Guilin

　　阳朔的田野上，金宝河像青罗带般曲折穿过，一
座座青山如玉笋般突兀而立，诗境的家园令世人感叹
不已。
　　In the landscape of Yangshuo, a green band
of Jinbao River winds forward among a world of
grotesque mountains. What a fairyland.

97. 报　春
Spring express
春の知ちせ
보춘
l'annonce de printemps
Die Frühlingsbotschaft
l'annunzio di primavera

　　遇龙河畔的田野一派
春意盎然。
　　Colors of spring
along Yulong River.

98.田间小石桥
Stone bridge
畑の小さい石橋
전간소석교
le petit pont dans les rizières
Die kleine Steinbrücke im Feld
il ponticello di pietra in mezzo ai campi

清晨、老人赶着牛儿往山野吃草。
In early morning,an old man is on his way to feed his cattle on grassland.

99.花 径
Blossom path
花の道

화경
un chemin au fleur
Der Blumenpfad

勤劳质朴的桂北劳动人民，他们正
走在一条充满阳光与鲜花，充满希望的
花径上。

Assiduously working people are
heading forward on a road of hope
full of sunshine and flowers.

100.金秋如画
A glance of golden autumn
画のような金秋
화같은 금수
I'automne pittoresque
Im malerischen Herbst
I'autunno d'oro pittoresco

金秋的桂北山村，绚丽多姿，
如诗如画。
It is a poetic scene of a
mountainous village of northern
Guangxi in autumn.

城 乡 建 筑

LOCAL ARCHITECTURAL CULTURE

　　"桂林山水甲天下，桂林风情醉万家。"这是人与自然的和谐，营造了甲天下的桂林。而具有民族特色的村寨民居、城镇建筑，又为桂林的美丽写下了那绚丽迷人的一笔。龙胜侗族的鼓楼和风雨桥，大圩古镇，兴坪渔村，恭城文庙，灌阳牌坊，壮、苗、瑶、侗寨的木屋以及那颇具桂北民居风情的青砖、青瓦和山墙，无不给人以古朴、优美、恬静的感受。

As expressed in the saying "Guilin's natural landscape ranks first in the world, and its customs intoxicate millions of households".Guilin is the harmonious merge of nature and humans. Added to the charm of Guilin is an indispensable touch of the local architectural culture. Some representatives including Dong people's Drum towers and wind-rain rridges, ancient town of DaXu, Fish village of Xinping, Wen Temple of GongCheng and the dwelling houses of local minorities.

101.杉湖日月双塔
 Fir Lake and its two towers
 杉湖の日塔と月塔
 삼호일월쌍탑
 les deux pagodes soleil-
lune dans le lac de sapin
 Beide Pagoden im Sha-See
 le pagode del sole e della
luna sul Laghetto dell'Abete

 流彩飞霞染湖杉，日月生辉展
英姿。待到烟花灿烂时，双塔显佛
光。
 Fir Lake is located in the
center of Guilin city. In the
dim light of night, its two
towers, namely Sun and Moon shine
together casting lights on the
flicking water.

102. 解放桥新姿
New look of Liberation Bridge
解放橋の新しい姿

해방교새모습
la nouvelle allure du pont de la libération
Die neue Befreiungsbrücke
l'aspetto del Ponte della Liberazione

解放桥始建于1939年,历史上曾经过多次维修。于1998年改建后的解放桥更加雄伟、壮观,其夜景更是流光溢彩,体现了桂林市新时代的风姿。

It was firstly built in 1939 and has been rebuilt for many times ever since including the large-scale reconstruction in 1998. It is most beautiful at night when standing on a blur of water and streams of lights.

103. 古 南 门
Ancient south city gate
古南門
고남문
la porte méridionale de I'ancienne cité
Das alte Südtor der Stadt

位于桂林市区榕湖北岸的古南门是桂林"唐城"的南大门，距今已有1300多年的历史。

It is located on the north bank of Banyan Lake. It was the south city gate of "Tang City" which has had a history of over 1300 years.

104.玻 璃 桥
Crystal bridge
ガテスの橋

유리교
le pont en verre
Die Glasbrücke
il Ponte di Vetro

横跨于榕湖上的玻璃桥，均由有机玻璃
制成，桥身通体晶莹、透亮，宛若玉桥，成为
桂林市一道奇特的风景线。

Overarching on the Banyan Lake, the
crystal bridge is made of organic glass.
The whole bridge is glittering and
translucent at night. It has become one
of Guilin's attractions of night.

105.花 桥
Flower bridge
花 橋

화교
le pont de fleur
Die Blumenbrücke
il Ponte dei Fiori

在七星公园正门灵剑江与东江汇合处，桥畔繁花似锦，小桥掩映于"满溪流水半溪花"之间，故名花桥，创建于宋朝，清嘉庆十九年重建。

A famous scenic spot in Guilin, the stone bridge is located at the juncture of Dong,jiang River and Ling,jian River at the front gate of Seven Star Park. The stone bridge is accompanied by the flowing waters and blossoms, from which it gets its name "Flower Bridge".

106. 宋　城
Song city
宋代の城
송성
la cité de la dynastie des SONGS
Die Song-Stadt
la Città di Song

宋城为桂林市新景"两江四湖"的第一站，
其仿宋的建筑风格及旅游接待服务把游客带到
了那段美好的历史。

It is the first stop of Guilin's newly
finished "Two Rivers and Four Lakes"
project. All the constructions are modeled
after Song's architectural style.

107.塔　山
Precious Pagoda Hill
塔山
탑산
la coline à la pagode
Der Pagodenberg
la Collina di Pagoda

位于漓江东岸，山上建有佛寿塔，实心、七层八角，为砖结构。

On the east bank of the Lijiang River and west bank of the Xiaodongjiang River in the southeast of Guilin, the hill is topped with a seven-storied, eight-pointed brick pagoda.

108.大圩古石板路
Daxu ancient town
大圩の古い石板道
대서고석로
le chemin en pièrre à DAXU
Der alte Fußweg aus Steinplatten
il sentiero lastricato antico di Daxu

　　大圩位于桂林市东南方向19公里处，建于公元前200年，现圩中仍保留有万寿桥、高祖庙、汉皇庙、古码头、会馆、古建筑等文物古迹。图为长达2.5公里的古石板路一角。

Daxu lies 19 km southeast to the Guilin city. It was built in 200 BC. There are many well-preserved relics such as Longevity Bridge, Gaozhu Temple, Hanhuang Temple, Ancient Port. The picture shows a part of the 2.5km ancient slate path.

109. 河湾古镇
River bay town
古镇と河湾
허완고진
un bourg antique au méandre de fleuve
Die alte Gemeinde an der Flußbiegung
il paesino antico di Hewan

河湾古镇即兴坪古镇,漓江到此拐了个弯,故名河湾古镇。其依山傍水、风景荟萃,粉墙乌瓦、石板小巷、古色古香,已有一千三百多年的历史。

River bay town, or Xinping ancient town get its name because it is situated at the place where Li jiang River takes a turn. Amidst verdant mountains and crystal-like waters, the scenic ancient town has a long history of over 1300 years, which can be sensed from the quaint brick houses and slate paths in the lanes.

110. 渔 村
Fish village
渔 村
어 촌
un village de pêcheurs
Das Fischerdorf
il villaggio dei pescatori

兴坪渔村约有400多年的历史,现村中建筑多为明清所建,青砖碧瓦、小巷纵横、庭院深深、房屋错落有致、户户雕梁画栋、屋檐飞禽走兽、图案雅致精巧,惟妙惟肖、古色古香。

Xinping fish village has been 400 years old in history. The architectures of the village were mostly built during Ming and Qing Dynasties. They are still well preserved with elegant, sloping rooftops, ornamental eaves, and narrow lanes set among the famous mountains and waters that are still there telling its history.

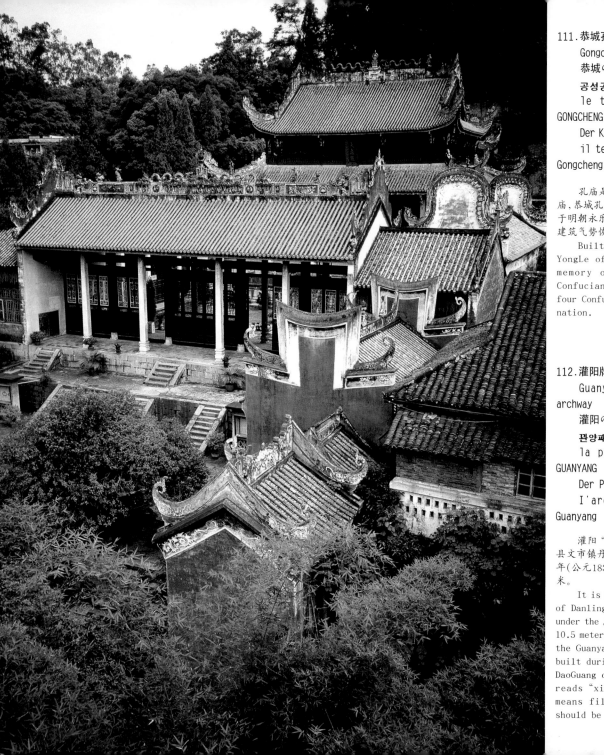

111. 恭城孔庙
Gongcheng Confucian temple

恭城の孔庙

공성공묘

le temple de confucius de GONGCHENG

Der Konfuziustempel in Gongcheng

il tempio di Confucianesimo di Gongcheng

　　孔庙是后人纪念和祭祀孔子的祠庙，恭城孔庙是我国四大孔庙之一，建于明朝永乐八年（公元1410年），整体建筑气势恢弘，文化蕴涵丰富。

　　Built in the eighth year of YongLe of Ming Dynasty for the memory of kongzi, Gongcheng Confucian temple is one of the four Confucian temples across the nation.

112. 灌阳牌坊
Guanyang ancient memorial archway

灌阳の牌坊（アーチ型の建物）

관양패방

la portique d'honneur de GUANYANG

Der Prachtbogen in Guanyang

I'arco commemorativo di Guanyang

　　灌阳"孝义可凤"牌坊，位于灌阳县文市镇丹岭村左侧，建于清道光十九年（公元1839年），通高10.5米，宽13.6米。

　　It is situated in the east side of Danling village, Wenshi county under the jurisdiction of Guanyang. 10.5 meters high, 13.8 meters wide, the Guanyang memorial archway was built during the reign of emperor DaoGuang of Qing Dynasty(1839).It reads "xiao yi ke feng", which means filial piety and loyalty should be admired.

113. 漓江源头秦家大院
The house of Qin family at the source of Lijiang River
灘江の源にある秦家の庭
이강원진가대원
la cour de la famille QIN à la sourse du fleuve Li
Der Qin-Hof in Xing' an
il Recinto della famiglia Qin situato alla sorgente del fiume Li

位于兴安县白石乡，该院保留着古朴的民间建筑艺术风格及文化韵味。

It is situated in Baishi town of Xing'an county. The house is authentic and well preserved and has been a living museum of the folk architecture style and culture.

114.龙胜吊桥

Longsheng suspension bridge

龍勝の吊り橋

룡성가등교

le pont suspendu de LONGSHENG

Die Hängebrücke in Longsheng

il ponte levatoio di Longsheng

　　龙胜桑江河上，吊桥数座，而此处乃为地势最险，景观奇特之处，有"天桥观猴"之景观。

　　It is one of the many suspension bridges over the Sangjiang River. It has got its most fame among others for its strategic situation and unique spectacle. It has the attraction "viewing monkeys from the sky bridge".

115. 侗家鼓楼
　　Dong drum tower
　　トン族の鼓楼
　　동가고루
　　une tour de tambour des DONGS
　　Der Trommelturm der Dong-
Nationalität
　　la pagoda di Tamburo della
minoranza Dong

　　侗家鼓楼是侗族的艺术体现，
多建于寨子中央。其有四方、亦有六
方结构。鼓楼均为木结构，不用一颗
铁钉、铁铆，十分牢固。集宝塔和亭
子的优雅于一身，壮观清雅、独具风
格。

　　Dong style Drum tower is
characteristic of Dong people's
art and culture. It is mostly
built in the center of the
village. Dong Drum tower can be
four-faceted or six-faceted. What
is striking about the tower is
that it totally denies the use
of any mental pitons or screws.
It performs the functions of both
tower and kiosk.

116. 鼓楼·水车
Drum towers and waterwheel
鼓楼と水車

고루·수차
une tour de tambour.une noria
Der Trommelturm und das Wasserrad
la pagoda di Tamburo e la ruota idraulica

鼓楼是侗族的标志和象征，是侗族人民集会、议事、娱乐的场所。其多为木结构的四方、飞檐、瓦顶、多层宫殿或宝塔式建筑，轻盈、优雅、雄浑而壮观。水车则是桂北地区劳动人民的一种古老的劳动工具，其利用水力推动车轮转动，从而进行灌溉或推磨。

Drum tower, symbol of Dong wisdom, provides a convenient place for fellow Dong people to gather for discussion and entertainments. Waterwheel has long been a tool of production among the people in the northern Guangxi area. It uses the flow of water to turn the wheel. It can be used to irrigate or pushing grinder.

117. 侗家风雨桥
Dong wind-rain bridge
トン家の風雨橋

동족풍어교
le pont du vent et de la pluie des DONGS
Die Brücke mit Dach der Dong-Nationalität
il ponte del vento e della pioggia della minoranza Dong

侗家风雨桥是侗族建筑中最具特色者，它是集桥、亭、廊三者为一体的独具风格的桥梁建筑。其多建于寨边溪河上，工程浩大，工艺复杂，式样独特。风雨桥是人们避风躲雨、乘凉休息的地方，也是侗族人民迎客送客的地方。

It is the symbol of Dong architectural culture. It is a roofed bridge with the multi-function as bridge, kiosk and corridor. It is mostly built outside of village over stream or river. The construction of such a bridge involves sophisticated skills and large number of resources. It provides shelter for Dong people and it is also the place where villagers receive and see off their guests.

118. 壮寨门楼·干栏屋
Zhuang stockaded village gateway and fence house
壮寨の門楼·干栏屋
장족문루 간란우
une tour portique d'un village des ZHUANGS
Torbogen und Bauernhaus der Zhuang-Nationalität
il padiglione della minoranza Zhuang e la casa di Ganlan

桂北地区的一些壮族居民，至今仍保留传统的干栏（"麻栏"）建筑。壮族"麻栏"建筑的村寨多依山而建，富有"人栖其上，畜禽其下"的楼居特点。

Some Zhuang people still keep the tradition of building and living in fence structures. It is generally a two-storied building built against hillside. The upper story is for people to live, the lower story is for stables.

119. 金坑红瑶吊角楼

Jinkeng Hong Yao projecting house

金坑红瑶族の吊角楼

금강홍요때이오죠루

une maison suspendue des YAOS à JINKENG

Das Bauernhaus der Yao-Nationalität

la torre d'angolo sospesa della minoranza Hong Yao di Jinkeng

　　龙胜红瑶寨子多为木结构的半边半角楼，通常是5柱3间，一边或两边有偏厦，大门多在上层屋头偏厦间。下层为灰房、牲口圈；上层正中为厅、房，正中央有火塘，是会客、饮食、日常活动的场所，偏房为厨房或贮藏室。

　　A typical Hong Yao house is usually a rectangular wood structure with five columns and three rooms. The gate is found on the side of the upper story which has the space for daily activities. Living room and bedrooms are in the middle. Side rooms are kitchen and warehouse. The lower story is for stables.

图书在版编目 (CIP) 数据

桂林风情／漓江出版社编 .—桂林：漓江出版社，2004.1
ISBN 7 - 5407 - 3065 - X

Ⅰ.桂... Ⅱ.漓... Ⅲ.桂林—概况 Ⅳ.K926.73

中国版本图书馆CIP数据核字（2003）第 108122 号

桂林风情 GUILIN FENGQING

编　　者／本社
策划责编／韦丹意
装帧设计／韦丹意
英文翻译／李　盈
日文翻译／刘　吉
韩文翻译／安光哲
德文翻译／吴裕康
法文翻译／卢存志
意文翻译／杨鸣生
出版发行／漓江出版社
社　　址／广西桂林市南环路159-1 号
邮政编码：541002
电话：(0773)2863971　2863978
传真：(0773)2802018
E-mail：1jcbs@public.glptt.gx.cn
印　　刷／深圳雅昌彩色印刷有限公司
开　　本／890×1240　1/24
印　　张／$5\frac{1}{3}$
版　　次／2004年1月第1版第1次印刷
印　　数／8000
ISBN 7-5407-3065-X/J·164
　　　　000050000

如有印装质量问题　请与工厂调换